Instaworld

Full of cute pics, facts and fun!

Scholastic Children's Books
Euston House, 24 Eversholt Street,
London NW1 1DB, UK

A division of Scholastic Ltd
London ~ New York ~ Toronto ~ Sydney ~ Auckland ~ Mexico City ~ New Delhi ~ Hong Kong

Published in the UK by Scholastic Ltd, 2017
© Scholastic Children's Books, 2017

ISBN 978 1407 17960 5

Printed and bound by Bell & Bain Ltd, United Kingdom

10 9 8 7 6 5 4 3 2 1

Papers used by Scholastic Children's Books are made from wood grown in sustainable forests.
www.scholastic.co.uk

Picture credits:

Front cover: (from top left–right) Jonathan Knowles/The Image Bank/ Getty Images; Axelle/Bauer-Griffin/FilmMagic/Getty Images; Photography by Alice Moles (from bottom left – right) Samir Hussein/WireImage/Getty Images; retales botijero/Moment Open/Getty Images; Nick Bubb www.imagecaptured.co.uk/Moment/Getty Images.
Back cover: (from top left-right) Lisa Wiltse/ Corbis Historical/Getty Images; Andrew Francis Wallace/ Toronto Star/Getty Images; Theo Wargo/ Staff/Getty Images Entertainment; Chris So/Toronto Star/Getty Images; FilmMagic / Contributor/ FilmMagic; KAREN BLEIER/AFP/Getty Images.
p4: Axelle/Bauer-Griffin/FilmMagic/Getty Images; p5: Zacharie Scheurer/Getty Images Entertainment/Getty Images; p6: Creative RF/ KristinaVF; p7 DEA / C. NOVARA/De Agostini/Getty Images; p8: Samir Hussein/WireImage/Getty Images; p9: Photography by Alice Moles; p10 Jeff Spicer/Getty Images Entertainment/Getty Images; p11: Samir Hussein/Getty Images Entertainment/Getty Images; p12: Copyright Crezalyn Nerona Uratsuji/Getty Images; p13: Ray Tamarra/GC Images/Getty Images p14: Cindy Ord/Getty Images Entertainment/Getty Images; p15: Jacopo Raule / Contributor/ GC Images; p16: Nick Bubb www.imagecaptured.co.uk/Moment/Getty Images; p17: Tony Barson/FilmMagic/Getty Images; p18: Gilbert Carrasquillo / Contributor/Getty Images Entertainment;p19: Larry Busacca / Staff/ Getty Images Entertainment; p20: Ricardo Siqueira/Brazil Photos/LightRocket/Getty Images; p21: Vera Anderson/WireImage/Getty Images; p22: Ben A. Pruchnie/Getty Images Entertainment/Getty Images; p23: Kevin Winter/Getty Images Entertainment/Getty Images; p24: MIGUEL MEDINA/AFP/Getty Images; p25: Jeff Spicer/Getty Images Entertainment/Getty Images; p26: KAREN BLEIER/AFP/Getty Images; p27: Kyodo News / Contributor/Kyodo News; p28: David M. Benett / Contributor/ Getty Images Entertainment; p29: Scott Legato/ Getty Images Entertainment/Getty Images; p30: FilmMagic / Contributor/ FilmMagic; p31: David M. Benett / Contributor/ Getty Images Entertainment; p32: Lisa Wiltse/Corbis Historical/Getty Images; p33: Tino Soriano; p34: Pablo Cuadra / Contributor/ WireImage; p35: Neil Mockford/Alex Huckle / Stringer/ GC Images; p36: Image Source/ Getty Images; p37: Jun Sato/GC Images/Getty Images; p38: Epsilon/Getty Images Entertainment/Getty Images; p39: Maarten de Boer/Getty Images Portrait/Getty Images; p40: Pascal Le Segretain/Getty Images Entertainment/Getty Images; p41: retales botijero/Moment Open/Getty Images; p42: Chris So/Toronto Star/Getty Images; p43: Paul Zimmerman / WireImage/Getty Images; p44: George Pimentel/WireImage/Getty Images; p45: Kevin Winter/Getty Images Entertainment/Getty Images; p46: David M. Benett / Contributor/Getty Images Entertainment; p47: The Washington Post/Getty Images; p48: Frank Bienewald/ LightRocket/Getty Images; p49: Andrew Francis Wallace/ Toronto Star/Getty Images; p50: Andreas Rentz/Getty Images Entertainment/Getty Images; p51: Gary Gershoff/ WireImage/ Getty Images; p52: Barcroft/ Barcroft Media/ Getty Images; p53: Dave J Hogan/Getty Images Entertainment/Getty Images; p54: Karwai Tang/WireImage/ Getty Images; p55: Larry Busacca/ Getty Images Entertainment/Getty Images; p56: Kevin Mazur / Contributor/ WireImage; p57: Jonathan Knowles/The Image Bank/ Getty Images; p58: KARIM SAHIB/AFP/ Getty Images; p59: DEA / G. CIGOLINI/De Agostini/ Getty Images; p60: ALBERTO PIZZOLI / Staff/ AFP; p61: Digital Camera Magazine/ Future/ Getty Images; p62: Von Rosenschilde/Ovoworks / Contributor/ The LIFE Images Collection; p63: Shirlaine Forrest/Getty Images Entertainment/Getty Images; p64: Edward Berthelot / Contributor/Getty Images Entertainment; p65: Ben A. Pruchnie/Getty Images Entertainment/Getty Images; p66: Flowerphotos/ Universal Images Group/Getty Images; p67: C Flanigan/FilmMagic/Getty Images; p68: Christopher Polk/ACM2016 / Contributor/ Getty Images Entertainment; p69: Mauricio Alanis/ Moment Mobile/Getty Images; p70: Dave M. Benett / Contributor/ WireImage; p71: Neilson Barnard/ Getty Images Entertainment/Getty Images; p72: Tim Graham / Contributor/ Getty Images News; p73: David McNew/Getty Images News/ Getty Images; p74: Jamie McCarthy/Getty Images Entertainment/Getty Images; p75: Anthony Harvey/Getty Images Entertainment/Getty Images; p76: Dave J Hogan / Contributor/ Getty Images Entertainment; p77: Jun Sato / Contributor/ WireImage; p78: ullstein bild / Contributor/ ullstein bild; p79: Lisa Wiltse/ Corbis Historical/Getty Images; p80: Kevin Mazur / Contributor/ Getty Images Entertainment; p81: Getty Images / Stringer/Getty Images Entertainment; p82: Joerg Koch / Stringer/ Getty Images News; p83: TPG / Contributor /Getty Images News; p84: Theo Wargo / Staff/Getty Images Entertainment; p85: Barry King / Contributor/ Getty Images Entertainment; p86: CHRIS DELMAS / Stringer/ AFP; p87: Roberto Machado Noa / Contributor/ LightRocket; p88: David M. Benett / Contributor/ Getty Images Entertainment; p89: Fred Duval / Contributor/ FilmMagic; p90: Marka / Contributor/ Universal Images Group; p92: PETIT Philippe / Contributor/ Paris Match; p93: Steve Granitz / Contributor/ WireImage; p94: Mike Coppola / Staff/ Getty Images Portrait; p95: Alison Gootee; p96: Tom Dulat / Stringer/ Getty Images News.

Every effort has been made to ensure that this information is correct at the time of going to print. Any errors will be corrected upon reprint.

Instaworld

Full of cute pics, facts and fun!

SCHOLASTIC

#singer #songwriter #weloveZayn #OneDirection #solo
#livemusic #concert #performer #actionshot

Five facts about Zayn:

1. His birthday is 12th January, 1993.
2. His favourite song is 'Thriller' by Michael Jackson.
3. He can play the triangle.
4. 'Zayn' is his stage name. His real name is spelled 'Zain'.
5. He has designed most of his tattoos himself.
   So creative!

Gigi Hadid

#fashion #model #strong #style #Berlin #Germany #blackandwhite #fashionshow #catwalk

Social stats

Facebook likes: over 3.5 million

Twitter followers: over 3 million

Instagram followers: over 25 million

Loving Labrador

#playful #friendly #adorable #dog #lab #puppy #instacute
#animalsofinstagram #instapup #dogsofinstagram

Did you know?

This is a Labrador retriever puppy – this breed is
known for being kind, intelligent and trusting.

Beautiful beach

#sun #sea #sand #palmtrees #relax #calm #happy
#100happydays #paradise #holiday #bluesky #travel

"Life is better at the beach."

Superstar Jen

Jennifer was the highest paid actress in the world in 2015 *and* 2016! #achievement

Jennifer Lawrence

#premiere #powerful #cool #actress #glamorous
#London #HungerGames #stylish #smiles #throwback

#food #pretty #colourful #delicious #instafood #icing
#hungry #decoration #baking #yum #hearts #flowers

Colourful cupcakes!

"Friends are like sprinkles on
the cupcake of life."

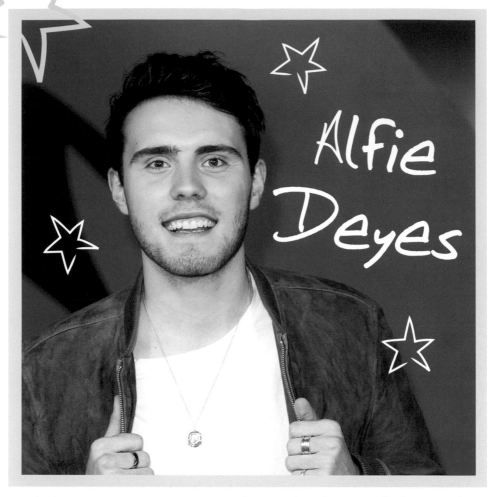

Alfie Deyes

#vlogger #creator #youtuber #cheeky #stylish #cool
#redcarpet #LeicesterSquare #premiere

Alfie's vlogging channels are:

- PointlessBlog
- PointlessBlogVlogs
- PointlessBlogGames

Did you Know?

Alfie can solve a Rubik's cube in under a minute!

Superstar Zoe!

Zoe has over 15 million subscribers across her two YouTube channels!

Zoe Sugg

#vlogger #creator #youtuber #throwback #makeup
#smiles #goals #teenawards #tbt

All you
need is
Love!

#happy #bunny #fluffy #cute #friendly #instacute #love
#animalsofinstagram #instaanimals #rabbitsofinstagram

Fluffy fact:

Baby rabbits are called 'kits'.

Taylor Swift

#NewYorkCity #throwback #style #swifties #weloveTaylor
#music #walking #happy #smile

Instafact:

Five of Taylor Swift's photos made it into the ten
most popular Instagram pictures of 2015, three
of which featured her adorable cat, Meredith.

Daniel Radcliffe

#actor #photoshoot #beard #style #HarryPotter
#NewYork #studio #navy #stripes

Did you know?

Daniel's favourite book in
the Harry Potter series is
*Harry Potter and the
Prisoner of Azkaban.*

#actress #singer #talented #crown #happy #Capri #Italy
#flowers #summer #travel #fashion #colour #inspiring

ZENDAYA

Cool fact:

Zendaya's name means 'to give
thanks'. Her motto is "Don't
forget to smile!"

Cute kitten!

#mini #tabby #adorable #surprised #awwww #kitten
#catsofinstagram #catgram #instacute #instaanimals

Tabby facts:

A tabby isn't a breed of cat – it refers to the pattern on its coat.

Tabby cats often have markings on their forehead that look like the letter 'm'. Can you spot it in the picture above?

Tabby cats are intelligent and affectionate.

Caspar Lee & Joe Sugg

#vloggers #youtubers #bff #Cannes #roadtrip #adventure #exciting #travel #film #Joe&CasparHittheRoad

Did you know?

Joe and Caspar used to live together and are still best friends. This photo was taken in Cannes to promote their film
Joe & Caspar Hit the Road.

Kendall Jenner

#supermodel #fashion #Jenner #throwback #sister
#famous #power #party #style

Facebook likes: over 15 million

Twitter followers: over 20 million

Instagram followers: over 65 million

Instafact:

Kendall is an Instagram pro. In 2015
the Instagram of her heart-shaped hair
design was the most liked image ever
on the platform, with 3.2 million likes.

Kylie Jenner

#Jenner #throwback #icon #sister #fierce #power #family #NewYork #fashion #gala #blackandwhite

Picture perfect Kylie!

Kylie has her own make-up brand, which is a huge success. It's so popular, in fact, that reportedly the first sale of her Lip Kit sold out in *one* minute!

Facebook likes: over 17 million

Twitter followers: over 18 million

Instagram followers: over 78 million

Wondrous waterfall

#IguazuFalls #nature #scenery #aweinspiring #travel #adventure #Brazil #wonder #amazing #beautiful

Iguazu Falls facts:

- The waterfalls are on the border between Brazil and Argentina.

- The name comes from the Guaraní language meaning 'great water'.

- Animals and birds spotted around the Falls include iguanas, deer and toucans.

Fun fact!

Anna's song – 'Cups (When I'm Gone)' – from *Pitch Perfect* became a hit and rose to No. 2 on the US Billboard's Pop Song chart.

Anna Kendrick

#Trollsfilm #PitchPerfect #star #actress #smile #pressconference #cool #singer #talented

John Boyega

#actor #StarWars #celebration #stylish #fun #happy
#exciting #London #onstage

Did you know?

Director JJ Abrams wanted to cast relative unknowns for his new Star Wars films. John Boyega, a 23-year-old Nigerian-born English actor, was one of the few who had what Abrams was looking for. Therefore, John was chosen as the lead role in *Star Wars: The Force Awakens*.

Daisy Ridley

#StarWars #teenchoice #star #style #actress #sparkle
#California #breakoutstar #award #sequins #cool

Venus and Serena Williams

![photo of Venus and Serena Williams shaking hands on a tennis court]

#tennis #superstars #sisters #winning #family #strong
#power #competition #goals #achievement

Super sisters!

The Williams sisters have a combined total of 9 Olympic medals.

Tom Daley

#diver #sport #stylish #awardceremony #redcarpet #star
#teamGB #strength #rolemodel

Did you know?

Tom became Britain's youngest diver to represent Great Britain at the Olympics – he qualified for Beijing when he was just 13 years old!

Perfect pandas ♡

#cute #pandas #mother #cub #zoo #Washington
#instacute #pandasofinstagram #family #love

Panda facts: ♡

- This is giant panda Mei Xiang and her cub Bei Bei playing in their enclosure 24th August, 2016 at the National Zoo in Washington, D.C. Bei Bei celebrated his first birthday 20th August, 2016.

- Baby pandas are born pink and measure about 15cm (about the size of a pencil!).

- A panda's diet is 99% bamboo.

☆ Happy birthday! ☆

This is a picture of Pata, a female sea otter kept at an aquarium in Osaka, Japan, who was given a special birthday cake made of ice for her 20th birthday on 28th June, 2016. Twenty years for an otter is roughly equivalent to 80 years in human terms!

Otterly adorable

#cute #adorable #happy #otter #nature #amazing #love
#ottersofinstagram #birthday #100happydays #icecake

#singer #OneDirection #actor #boyband #superstar #cool #xfactor #London #fashion #launch #event

Social Stats

Facebook likes: over 14 million

Twitter followers: over 29 million

Instagram followers: over 18 million

Amazing Adele!

Adele's album *25* has sold over 15 million copies worldwide!

Adele x

#singer #songwriter #talented #inspiring #fierce #style
#funny #loveher #downtoearth #power #amazingvoice

Dan & Phil

#vloggers #creators #youtubers #pose #cool #trendy
#funny #friends #friendship #bff

Social stats

Dan

YouTube: over 600 million views

Twitter: over 4 million followers

Instagram: over 3.5 million followers

Phil

YouTube: over 400 million views

Twitter: over 3.5 million followers

Instagram: nearly 3 million followers

Jim & Tanya

#creators #youtubers #stylish #wife #husband #inlove
#smiles #inspiring #booklaunch #London

Instafact:

Despite having many prominent internet stars such as Zoella and Tyler Oakley at their wedding, the pair actually decided to *ban* social media at the event, saying on the invite: 'Rules: no vlogging, no Snapchat, no social media.' Jim said: "We wanted our wedding to be very intimate, very private. We share so much of our lives, and we wanted a day where we could just turn everything off."

YUMMY GUMMY BEARS

#food #sweets #colour #gummybears #delicious
#snack #yum #sweet #chewy #treat

GUMMY GIANT

The biggest gummy bear money can buy
is nearly 12 kilos.

"Always look for the rainbow after the rain."

Colours of the rainbow

#rainbow #wow #nature #aweinspiring #colour #travel
#clouds #Ireland #DiamondHill #ConnemaraNationalPark

Brooklyn Beckham

#cool #Beckham #famousfamily #fashion #Spain
#visit #travel #smile #stylish

Instafact:

When Brooklyn celebrated reaching one million followers on Instagram, he posted a hilarious video where his famous footballer dad, David Beckham, upstaged him by saying he had 52. Thankfully, Brooklyn saw the funny side later as he captioned the video: "Reached 1 million followers on my mum's birthday. Thank u guys so much #ismydadcoolerthanme."

Social stats

Facebook likes: nearly 10 million

Twitter followers: over 8 million

Instagram followers: over 5 million

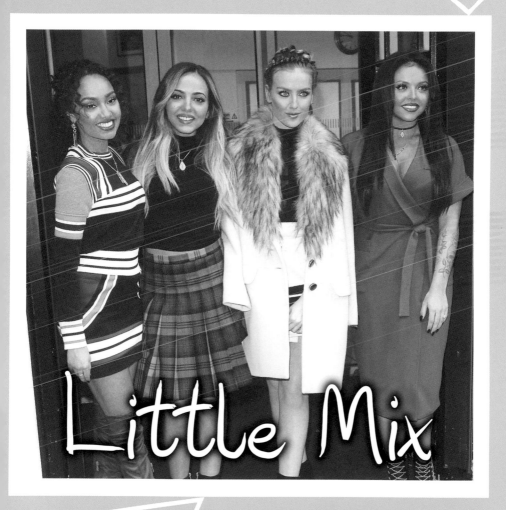

Little Mix

#girlband #singers #superstars #stylish #friends #power
#music #smiles #happy #London #attitude #fierce

clever ducks

A duck's top layer of feathers is highly waterproof. These feathers are so waterproof that when a duck dives underwater, the second layer of feathers stays totally dry!

Darling ducklings

#adorable #cute #ducklings #happy #yellow #fluffballs
#ducksofinstagram #instaanimals #100happydays

Selena Gomez

#popstar #Tokyo #stylish #airportchic #sunglasses #red
#star #actress #singer #travel #jetsetter

Did you know?

Selena met fellow star Demi Lovato
when they acted together in the 1992
TV show *Barney and Friends*.

Timberlake tip!

Justin has a secret to eating Oreo biscuits and milk.
He says you need to dunk the Oreo in the milk for
exactly seven seconds – making sure it doesn't go
too soggy or stay too hard.

Justin Timberlake

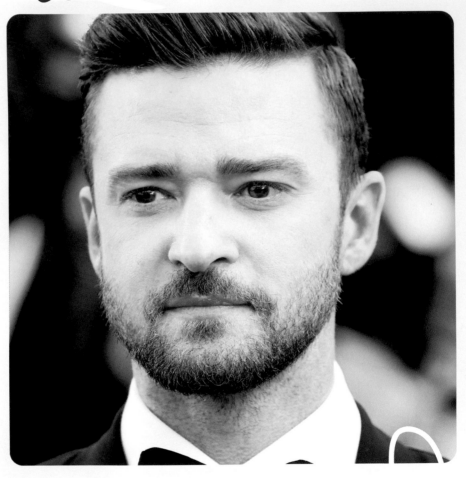

#Cannes #filmfestival #France #singer #star #music
#actor #redcarpet #style #poplegend

Amandla Stenberg

#HungerGames #teenstar #photoshoot #stylish #cool
#inspiring #empowering #actress #fashion #Utah

Inspiring Amandla

Amandla is a proud youth ambassador for the non-profit-making
charity No Kid Hungry, an organization devoted to ending child
hunger in America. She's also a supporter of Ubuntu Education
Fund, a non-profit organization that supports the education
of South African children.

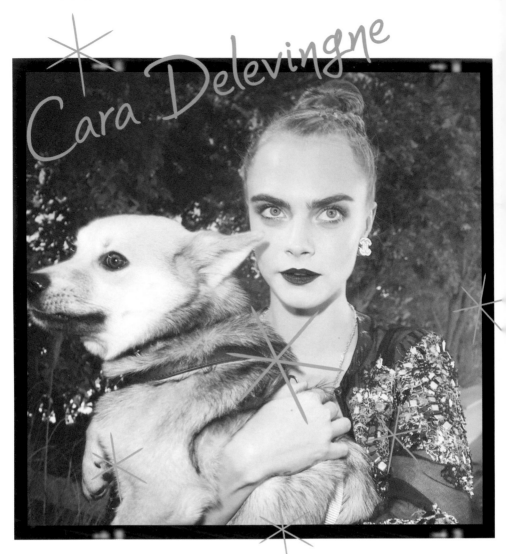

Cara Delevingne

#supermodel #Chanel #Parisfashionweek #sequins #cool
#Paris #France #instastar #funny #kooky #cutedog

Musical model!

In her spare time, Cara loves to
play the drums!

Did you know?

A group of pugs is called a 'grumble'.

Photogenic pug dog

#adorable #instacute #quirky #dressup #pug #pugdog
#pugsofinstagram #pugly #dressedupdogs

Piece of cake...

#rainbow #colours #frosting #yummy #creative #baking
#instafood #hungry #eatme #delicious #foodpics

Did you know?

20th July is International Cake Day. The
aim for this sweet summer holiday is to
spread friendship and love through cakes!

Funny fact!

When Joe was younger, he got his head stuck in a tambourine!

Joe Jonas

#EmpireStateBuilding #singer #songwriter #star
#Jonasbrother #DNCE #band #NewYork #actionshot

Zac Efron

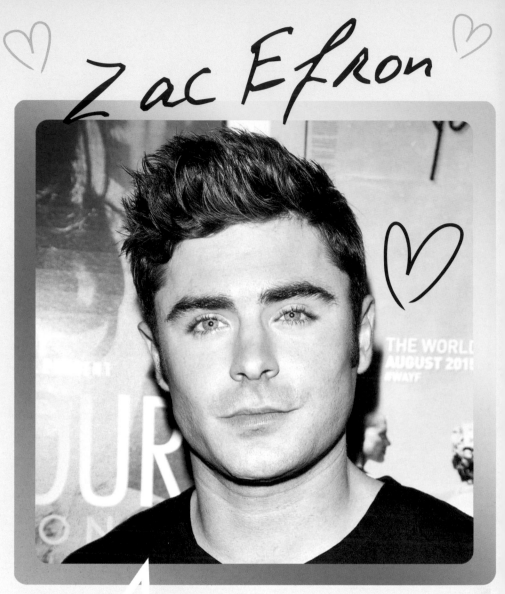

#filmstar #singer #HighSchoolMusical #actor #Toronto #afterparty #film #style

Social stats

Facebook likes: over 18 million

Twitter followers: over 13 million

Instagram followers: over 22 million

Did you know?

Ariana's favourite cereal is Cocoa Puffs and her favourite fruit is strawberries.

Ariana Grande

#singer #BillboardMusicAwards #performer #LasVegas
#stylish #routine #onstage #popstar #actionshot

Bella Hadid

#supermodel #posing #fashion #shoot #icon #party
#London #Londonfashionweek #glamour #sparkles

Did you know?

Bella used to be a professional horse rider. She said, "It taught me a lot about responsibility. You're up at 5:30 a.m. caring for and riding a huge animal. I would be at horse shows by myself for weeks, and I had to make sure I was on my game at all times."

FRESHLY BAKED COOKIES

#chocolate #soft #mouthwatering #delicious #baking
#eatme #yum #melting #instafood

Delicious discovery

Chocolate chip cookies were created by accident! In 1937 Ruth
Wakefield had run out of baker's chocolate for her famous
cookies, so used a bar of sweeter chocolate instead. She thought
it would melt completely but instead it only softened, leaving
chocolate pieces mixed in with the cookie. This way the
chocolate chip cookie was invented.

Breathtaking Mount Everest

#MountEverest #dramatic #stunning #scenery #nature
#mountain #snowy #shadow #cloud #beautiful

"Every mountaintop is within
reach if you just keep climbing..."

FLOWER POWER

"Be like a sunflower - stand
tall and follow the sun."

#sunflower #bluesky #nature #golden #happy #happiness
#growth #100happydays #flower #bright #standtall

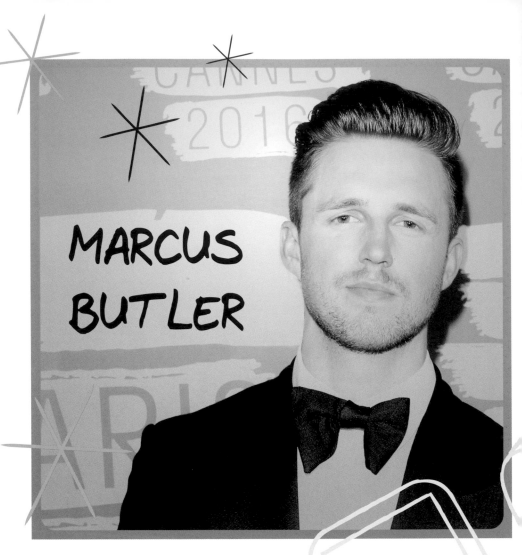

MARCUS BUTLER

#vlogger #musical #author #suit #blacktie #youtuber #bowtie #Cannes #style

SOCIAL STATS

YouTube views: over 370 million

Twitter followers: nearly 3 million

Instagram followers: over 3 million

Did you know?

'Tyler' isn't his first name – it's his middle name! His first name is actually 'Matthew'.

Tyler Oakley

#webbyawards #VIP #vlogger #youtuber #author #happy
#activist #smiling #funny

Cutie-pie creatures

#micropig #dog #bff #snuggles #pigsofinstagram
#animalsofinstagram #instacute #dogsofinstagram

Best buds!

This micropig and dog get on so well
that they eat, sleep and play together!

Beautiful ballet shoes

#enpointe #dancing #graceful #EnglishNationalBallet
#flexible #hardwork #determination #strength #elegant

Determined dancers

Ballet dancers wear special shoes called 'pointe shoes'
so they can dance on their toes. This is an incredibly
hard skill to master and takes years of training.

Niall Horan

#socceraid #football #charity #OneDirection #sport
#teamplayer #blue #singer #inspiring #fundraiser

Did you know?

In this photo, Niall is playing football for Soccer Aid,
a charity event that raises money for UNICEF UK to
help them build a better world for children.

Viral star

Shawn became famous by posting awesome six-second clips on Vine. Since his first video in 2013, he's reached about five million followers!

Shawn Mendes

#musician #concert #NewYork #guitar #skills #star #performing #lights #stage #viral #actionshot

Rita Ora

#singer #superstar #talkshow #smile #sparkle #happy
#100happydays #throwback #popstar

Did you know?

Rita Ora absolutely loves hot sauce and has even admitted to putting it on cereal, fruit and pretty much anything else you can think of. It's even been said she carries a bottle in her bag for emergencies!

Ice-cream inspo

Unusual flavours

The following weird ice-cream flavours have all actually been made:

1. Crocodile egg ice cream
2. Bacon ice cream
3. Garlic ice cream
4. Charcoal ice cream
5. Lobster ice cream

6. Turkey ice cream
7. Curry ice cream
8. Jellyfish ice cream
9. Sweet potato ice cream
10. Smoked salmon ice cream

GALLOPING WONDER

#Arabianhorse #gallop #awe #speed #majestic
#horsesofinstagram #horse #beauty #elegant

Did you know?

The Arabian horse is one of the oldest breeds
in history, dating back over 4,000 years!

A scattering of shells

#cockleshells #sand #pretty #patterns #sea #collection #soundofthesea #shells #stripes

Amazing armour

Shells help to protect, shield and camouflage the animals inside them.

Lily-Rose Depp

#model #actress #star #smiling #happy #fun #France #style #stylish #cool

Did you know?

Lily-Rose grew up in Paris and is fluent in French!

Did you know?

Trees that lose their leaves
in autumn are called
deciduous trees.

Falling leaves

#nature #autumn #colours #seasonschange #fall #falling
#orange #yellow #beautiful #leaves

The Siamese is one of the oldest breeds of house cat. They came from Thailand (which used to be called Siam), where they were prized members of the royal family, and images of them on manuscripts go as far back as 1350.

Pretty kitty

#Siamese #gorgeous #cutie #blueeyes #cat #instacute #catsofinstagram #animalsofinstagram #kitten

Justin Bieber

#singer #vfestival #superstar #performer #beliebers
#actionshot #performing #popstar #youtubesensation

Did you Know?

Justin once auctioned a lock of his hair
for charity. It raised over £25,000.

Karlie Kloss

#model #pose #Paris #France #fashionweek #inspiring #cool #strong #stylish #smile

Did you know?

Karlie founded a summer camp called 'Kode with Klossy' to teach 13 to 18-year-old girls how to code. By teaching this useful life skill, Karlie is inspiring girls and helping to develop their potential!

Louis Tomlinson

#star #Monaco #MonteCarlo #shades #OneDirection
#boyband #singer #performer #smile #sunshine

Social Stats

Facebook Likes: over 10 million

Twitter followers: over 23 million

Instagram followers: over 11 million

Juicy strawberries

#fruit #red #delicious #nature #readytoeat #eatme
#seasonal #instafood #yum #savemeone

Ripe and ready!

Strawberries are the first fruit to ripen in early summer. When they are ripe they are bright red, juicy and very sweet - just like these ones!

Beyoncé ♡

#MTV #VMAs #singer #superstar #independentwoman
#icon #style #fierce #powerful #inspiring

Superstar Beyoncé

Beyoncé was the first woman to win

six Grammy Awards

in one night.

Fun fact!

Katy Perry is actually a stage name. Katy's full name is Katheryn Elizabeth Hudson. Perry is her mother's maiden name.

Katy Perry

#popstar #unique #kooky #LasVegas #MGMGrand
#smiles #happy #music #exciting #superstar #colourful

Perfect pool

#Mexico #swimming #pool #luxury #chill #calm #holiday
#paradise #relax #dreams #adventure #travel #sunshine

Did you know?

This type of pool is called an infinity
pool because the water looks as if it
blends into the sea, stretching on
for ever...

Ice-cream dreams

Rupert's first ambition was to become an ice-cream man!
His dream was fulfilled when he bought an ice-cream van
with his Harry Potter earnings. He has been known
to drive it around his local villages!

Rupert Grint

#actor #HarryPotter #RonWeasley #magic #throwback
#London #PostmanPatpremiere #redcarpet #smile

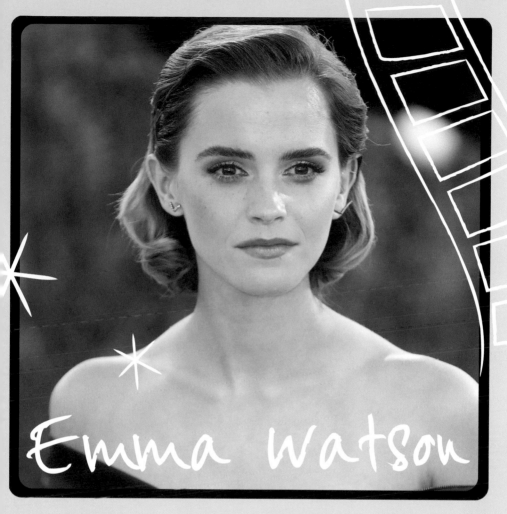

Emma Watson

#actress #HarryPotter #Hermione #stylish #inspiration
#power #fierce #elegant #icon

Inspiring Emma

Emma is Women Goodwill Ambassador for
the UN, and dedicates her time towards the
empowerment of young women.

Lovely lambs

#countryside #lambs #nature #instacute #happy #playing
#exploring #flowers #field #spring #lambsofinstagram

Frolicking fact!

Lambs are born in the spring, when the warmer days and regular
rainfall mean plants and grass grow really well. Sheep are
herbivores, which means they only eat vegetation such as grass -
so they need lots of it to grow up big and healthy!

Diving dolphin

#nature #scenic #wildlife #sea #wow #jump #splash #tail #dolphin #water #powerful #animalsofinstagram

Clever creatures

Compared to most animals, dolphins are very intelligent. Not only do they have their own cultures, but they may also have names for each other – using distinctive whistles to call to their friends.

Shailene Woodley

#actress #talkshow #stylish #happy #cool #smiles
#TheFaultinOurStars #Divergentseries

Fun fact!

Shailene, in reference to her fame, has said:
"If I didn't have acting, I would be just as happy...
I would probably be a herbalist, or maybe I would
open a fruit stand on a Hawaiian island."

Ansel Elgort

#MTV #VMAs #actor #stylish #edgy #DJ
#Divergentseries #TheFaultinOurStars

Did you know?

Not only is Ansel a superstar actor, he's
also a highly successful DJ. He works
under the name 'Ansolo'.

Social stats

Facebook likes: over 10 million
Twitter followers: over 23 million
Instagram followers: over 11 million

Liam Payne

#singer #songwriter #London #BritAwards #O2Arena
#OneDirection #trendy #style

Liam Hemsworth

#actor #HungerGames #strikeapose #redcarpet #suit #moviestar #smile #smiling

Brave Brothers

Liam is Australian and was born in Melbourne. He moved to America (along with famous actor brother, Chris) to pursue his acting dreams.

Happy hedgehogs

#animals #nature #wildlife #instacute #hedgehogs
#family #animalsofinstagram #hedgehogsofinstagram

Prickly fact!

Hedgehogs get their name because of their foraging habits. They root through hedges and other undergrowth in search of their favourite foods — small creatures such as insects, worms, centipedes, snails, mice, frogs and snakes. As they do this they make noises a bit like a pig's grunt — thus, the name hedgehog.

Pizza perfect

#mozzarella #herbs #fancy #mouthwatering #eatme
#pizza #slices #authentic #tomato #instafood

Top ten weird pizza toppings:

1. Marshmallows
2. Raspberries
3. Hamburgers
4. Chocolate sauce
5. Cauliflower

6. Popcorn
7. Granola
8. Sunflower Seeds
9. Cranberries
10. Fried egg

Sofia Richie

#singer #actress #hairgoals #edgy #style #icon #fashion #fashionable #blackandwhite

Instafact:

Sofia loves dogs and has her own adorable French bulldog named Cairo Richie. She calls him her 'little nugget' and he even has his own Instagram account!

Sophie Turner

#actress #redhead #sunnies #cool #talented #fashion
#BritishSummerTimeFestival #HydePark #London

Despite her signature red locks, Sophie's actually
a natural blonde. She dyes her hair the trademark
auburn for her role as Sansa in *Game of Thrones*.

"Life isn't about waiting for the storm to pass... It's about learning to dance in the rain."

Under my umbrella

#rain #umbrellas #colourful #pattern #pretty #unusual
#Fujian #China #art #decoration

#smiling #performing #superstar #inspiration #umbrella
#casual #happy #RiRi #popstar #style

Superstar RiRi

Rihanna's song 'Umbrella' was a huge success and shot straight to the top in 13 countries. What's more amazing is that it remained at No. 1 in the UK for 10 weeks!

Funfairs and Ferris wheels

#Ferriswheel #lights #rain #reflections #funfair #pretty
#rides #colourful #picturesque

Ferris fact!

The Ferris wheel is named after its inventor, George
Washington Gale Ferris, Jr. It was made in 1893 for the
Chicago World's Fair and was 80.4 metres high!

Josh Hutcherson

#actor #HungerGames #Peeta #suit #smart #smiles
#style #redcarpet #throwback #prankster

Prankster Peeta!

Josh is a bit of a prankster. He once hid a
full life-sized dummy in Jennifer Lawrence's
trailer to scare her.

Willow and Jaden Smith

#siblings #brotherandsister #singers #rappers #supercool
#icons #unique #stylish #actor #actress

Super siblings!

Both Jaden and Willow have appeared as
on-screen kids to their real-life movie star dad
Will Smith. Willow appeared as Will's daughter
in *I Am Legend* and Jaden appeared as his son
in *The Pursuit of Happyness*.

Making waves

#waves #blue #wow #SantaMariaKey #clouds #sunrise
#tranquil #relaxing #100happydays #view

"Don't ever be afraid to make
some waves."

Ella Purnell

#floral #skirt #lipstick #smile #garden
#MissPeregrinesHomeforPeculiarChildren

Fun fact!

If Ella won the lottery, she
would buy an ostrich.

Margot Robbie

#actress #fierce #tiger #Gucci #thatdress #fashion #icon
#talented #cool #smile #happy

Did you know?

Margot Robbie's nickname from her family
is 'Maggot'!

Lazy days

#sleepy #cute #awww #tree #kitten #cats #purrfect #lazy #catnap #catsofinstagram #instacute

Did you know?

Cats can sleep up to 16 hours a day, and for older cats, it could even be up to 20 hours!

Relaxing Seal

#cutie #relaxed #adorable #instacute #seal #sea
#animalsofinstagram #sealsofinstagram

Super seals!

Seals can hold their breath underwater for longer
than most animals on the planet. For instance, female
elephant seals have been recorded holding their breath
for two hours and diving more than 4,000 feet!

Cheery Chocolate

#chocolate #yum #bliss #cocoa #delicious #happy #love #sweet #yummy #instafood #treat

Did you know?

Chocolate doesn't just taste great, but can be good for your happiness, too. Chocolate contains phenylethylamine (PEA), which encourages your brain to release feel-good endorphins. This is the same chemical that your brain creates when you feel like you're falling in love!

Eddie Redmayne

#dapper #suit #actor #amazing #blackandwhite #bowtie
#redcarpet #FantasticBeastsandWheretoFindThem

Did you know?

Eddie has help looking so dapper on the red carpet. He's
colour-blind so often asks his wife to pick out and
coordinate his outfits!

Maisie Williams

#kooky #quirky #stylish #actress #talented #cool
#smile #stripeyshirt #photoshoot #studio

Unique taste

Maisie's known for being quirky and her food tastes are no different. She once said in an online interview that her perfect sandwich would contain cold chicken, salt-and-vinegar crisps and tomato ketchup... Interesting choice!

My cup of tea

#tea #cake #cuppa #flowers #teapot #teacup #pretty
#yummy #calming #scones #cute

Tea time!

There are thousands of different kinds
of tea in the world, making it the second
most popular drink after water!

Out with a bang!

#fireworks #wow #celebrations #sky #colourful #bang
#pretty #lightupthesky #spectacular #power

"We all have fireworks within
us, waiting to explode."